ideals®
EASTER

Now comes spring and Eastertime!
What a cause for lilting rhyme—
when the earth from winter's nap
sheds somber shawl for bright green wrap.
—Virginia Borman Grimmer

ideals®
Nashville, Tennessee

The feet that slid so long on sleet are glad to feel the ground.
—RALPH WALDO EMERSON

We Wait for Spring
John Greanleaf Whittier

'Tis the noon of springtime, yet never a bird
in the wind-shaken elm or the maple is heard;
for green meadow grasses, wide levels of snow,
and blowing of drifts where the crocus should blow.
Where windflower and violet, amber and white,
on south-sloping brooksides should smile in the light
o'er the cold winter beds of their late-waking roots,
the frosty flake eddies, the ice crystal shoots.
And longing for light under wind-driven heaps,
round the boles of the pinewood, the ground laurel creeps,
unkissed of the sunshine, unbaptized of showers,
with buds scarcely swelled, which should burst into flowers!
We wait for thy coming, sweet wind of the south,
for the touch of thy light wings, the kiss of thy mouth,
for the yearly evangel thou bearest from God—
resurrection and life to the graves of the sod!

NEARLY SPRING *by John Sloane. Image © John Sloane*

The Cardinal's Song
Lorna Volk

The cardinal, with crimson wings,
waits for springtime as he sings—
for signs of life as yet unseen,
for tender grass and leaves of green.
He waits for bright and sunny skies,
for daffodils and butterflies;
he waits with all his forest friends
for warmer days when winter ends.

The World Awakening
Lorna Volk

To see the world awakening—
how lovely it can be,
as newborn colors touch the earth
and sparkle on the sea,
as flowers open trustingly
their petals one by one
and start the day in bright array
with faces to the sun.
To see the world awakening—
no pleasure can compare
when nature is in harmony
and spring is in the air!

Early Morning Surprise
Faye Adams

One misty morning
a short time ago,
a bright purple nose
pierced the snow.
I felt a leap within
    my breast
as I beheld its snowy nest;
and with joy,
my attention focused
on the shining eye
of spring's first crocus.

Showtime
Norma West Linder

Called "ears of the earth"
by First Nation people,
crocuses—
sunshine yellow,
luminous white,
delicate mauve—
thrust loveliness
through dingy earth
patched here and there
with April snow,
an ever-welcome
springtime show.

The Root of the Matter
Hal Borland

This is the season when one can listen only so long to any recital of the world's shortcomings. Then we have to get outdoors and see the world itself. There we know that, though a thousand things may be wrong, a million things are right.

What are some of them? They are so obvious it seems foolish to list them. Water still runs downhill, making brooks that sing. Grass sends up new shoots, greening hillside and meadow. Robins migrate and strut about the lawn and sing their mating call. Daffodils swell in bud and open petals that are more yellow than gold. Weeping willows turn green and graceful while maples put forth their wine-red blossoms. The new-turned earth of field or garden is still full of fertility. Ferns send up pale green fiddleheads. Bees begin their summer's search. The man of the soil prepares his fields and sorts his seeds, knowing that the earth is eager to nourish another crop.

These are simple, obvious things. They may be seen any April, along with the swelling of apple buds and the opening of tulips. If they happened but once in ten years, we would wait breathless for their coming and put aside all other worries for their arrival. Instead, they are commonplace and taken for granted while we bandy words and dispute ideas. The trouble is, the words are too often rootless, and the ideas are sterile. Who can command a man to plant hemp and harvest wheat—or to plant hate and harvest peace? Who can command a lark to sing the oriole's song?

The world is in order, out where ideas have roots. April invites a conference on an open hillside to investigate the state of things at their common source.

Photograph © Elena Elisseeva/Shutterstock

Through My Window

Spring Has Sprung

Pamela Kennedy

I have a great respect for gardeners. In fact, some of my best friends are passionate about gardening. As spring approaches, they dream of hanging baskets overflowing with geraniums and dripping with lobelia, fuchsias, and trailing ivy. They order truckloads of bark and flats of seedlings and become giddy over every little crocus and narcissus that pokes its sturdy head above the earth. They wax poetic about variegated aspidistra and the profusion of poppies they anticipate. I, on the other hand, put away my silk mums, birds of paradise, and bromeliads and dust off my designer hyacinths and tulips. It is spring after all!

This is not to say I don't appreciate a beautiful garden. Just last April I drove north of our home in Seattle to enjoy the Skagit Valley Tulip Festival comprising over a million blossoms carpeting about 100 acres in bands of rainbow hues. It was truly breathtaking. Then, in May, while on a trip to Great Britain, I spent many happy hours wandering the verdant eighty-acre grounds of world-famous Bodnant Garden in Conwy, Wales. I love all manner of beautiful flowers. The problem is I just can't seem to cultivate them with any degree of success.

And I did not reach this conclusion without many years of experience and experimentation. During my husband's twenty-eight-year Navy career, I had an opportunity to fail at gardening in a variety of locations and climes. Squirrels and deer feasted on my daffodils in Virginia. Bunnies chowed down on my tulips in Wisconsin. I watched my petunias do poorly in Rhode Island and my violets shrivel in San Diego. Even in Hawaii—where, I'm told, no one can fail to grow things—I set out rows of healthy bedding plants only to find them the next morning munched down to the roots by slugs and snails.

"Put jar lids filled with beer in your flower beds," my neighbor suggested. "That will take care of them."

Oh, that worked like a charm. I had the happiest slugs in the Pacific, chomping my marigolds and impatiens between swigs of beer. Indoor plants, outdoor plants, plants that sit on screened porches—all seem to sense when I'm around and uniformly fail to thrive. I have over-watered and under-watered and managed to do in everything from orchids to succulents. Some have lasted a few months, but then, the telltale signs of impending doom begin to show up—darkening leaves, dried out buds, drooping stems, dropping blossoms. So what was I to do?

At first I resisted the idea of false foliage and fake flowers. Wouldn't they just scream "Tacky!"? But at my dentist's office one day, I remarked about the beautiful green plants stationed around the waiting room.

"Yep, they're fakes," announced the receptionist.

"Seriously?" I approached one and checked it out. It looked so robust, with thick stalks and glossy dark green leaves.

"I just take 'em out back, give 'em a good spraying with the hose every six months or so, and then shine up their leaves with a little almond oil now and then. Piece of cake! Oh, and check out these beauties." She motioned to a gorgeous arrangement of orchids "blooming" profusely from a pottery bowl on the corner of the counter. "False as some of the teeth around here!" she whispered conspiratorially.

That did it. Right after my appointment I headed off to the floral decor store, where I strolled between aisles and piles of everything from pussy willows to peonies. There were twining vines of all varieties, potted plants, and even seven-foot-tall ficus trees! It was a faux gardener's paradise!

Ever since that day, I have filled my home with a beautiful abundance of artificial (I prefer the term "ever-living") plants. They never die or disappoint me. When I go on vacation, they don't pine or wither. Their eager little leaves and blossoms greet me with enduring brightness upon my return. No more wondering how dry or damp to keep the soil. In fact, no more soil!

I realize there are those for whom an artificial plant is akin to sacrilege. And I suspect some faithful readers are already clucking their tongues and shaking their heads in disapproval, but that's okay. Spring, for me and you, just looks a little bit different.

Enjoy your buds and bulbs. Relish sinking your hands into the fertile loam of your garden. Bless each little seed and seedling that nestles in your soil as you wait for it to burst forth in flowery profusion. As for me and my house, we will serve up the charlatans of the floral world and delight in their unchanging and eternal beauty, dusting them gently now and then; occasionally perking up their petals; and, every once in a while, polishing their leaves with just a touch of almond oil.

Spring Versus Cleaning
Vera Keevers Smith

My neighbors hang their blankets out
and put the winter dust to rout.
With brush and mop, with work and din,
their houses shine without, within.
For shame that I, who have work too,
should sit and dream the way I do
and greet again each little face
of pansies with their pensive grace
and think of lilacs yet to come,
the snowy bough of pear and plum.
The slow unfolding leaf of tree
is always miracle to me.
I cannot work with mop or broom
when earth is coming into bloom,
but needs must watch the shining glory
as spring retells her ancient story.

Spring Called Me
Garnett Ann Schultz

Spring called me from my
    work today
to climb a far-off hill.
Because I heard a robin sing
and saw each daffodil,
my mind just wandered off;
it seemed my heart was far away,
and quickly I was off and gone
where little streamlets play.
Spring put a song within my heart
and laughter in my eyes;
for spring held naught but
    wondrous joy
and pleasant, sweet surprise.

I picked a smiling violet
and loved its gentle charms;
I saw a precious nesting bird
within the oak tree's arms.
Spring called me from my
    work today
and taught me how to dream
and left me in a happy mood
beside a laughing stream.
I loved this early April morn,
the blue skies overhead,
when springtime called me
    from my work
and bid me play instead.

Photograph © Friedrich Strauss/Gap Photos Ltd.

Spring Cleaning

Mary Weeks

I meant to do my work today. The stove needed cleaning, ironing was piled high, floors needed mopping, beds wanted fresh linen. I needed to study psychology and do my math for class, but I figured I could apply my psychology by socializing with others and apply my math by counting the dogwood blossoms, daffodils, tulips, and weeds in my garden!

Lydia O. Jackson wrote, "Although the calendar says spring, and birds sing every minute, it isn't spring unless your heart removes the winter in it." Hang on to the dead, cold signs of winter, and you cannot possibly enjoy the new life of spring that always comes at just the right moment for us. Pack away the quilts, clean out the fireplaces, put up the winter coats, and put away winter for another year.

Golden daffodils shout the good news of spring and new life while the tiny crocus breaks through the final remnant of snow to tell us the glorious season of renewal and rebirth is arriving! Grass turns green, birds build nests in trees, dogs dig up the soft soil of the soon-to-be garden, sunshine awakens us a bit earlier, and evening extends its hours a bit longer. It is spring! There is new life, new energy, new enthusiasm as freshness in the soft breezes blow and hope that this world will be a bit better blossoms.

I love the springtime! The freedom from heavy coats and often heavy thoughts; the extra spring in my walk; the songs of birds, blooms of flowers, and laughter of children kept inside for too long; the babbling of an open creek; the beauty of a sunrise or sunset that even the poorest can enjoy. I love spring . . . friendly people out walking and talking, dogs barking at cats in trees, woods turning green, softly falling showers, students on spring break, the end of a school year coming into sight. Spring means Easter, the sound of a woodpecker on the roof, and the thrill of being free to enjoy God's beauty.

The psalmist wrote, "What is man, that thou art mindful of him?" (Psalm 8:4). When I survey what God has created for us to enjoy and when I remember His love, I truly stand amazed in the presence of God and thank Him for the beauty of the earth, for spring, for the joy of knowing Christ. I thank Him for the birds, the trees, the rocks, the warm sun, the broken soil, the holidays, the flowers, and all that comes with this season called spring.

I meant to do my work today, but instead I took time off to sample the beginnings of a new season and found them to be more important than routine chores—at least for this day.

Photograph © Pernilla Bergdahl/GAP Photos Ltd.

Loveliest of Trees
A. E. Housman

Loveliest of trees, the cherry now
is hung with bloom along the bough
and stands about the woodland ride,
wearing white for Eastertide.
Now, of my threescore years and ten,
twenty will not come again,
and take from seventy springs a score,
it only leaves me fifty more.
And since, to look at things in bloom,
fifty springs are little room,
about the woodlands I will go
to see the cherry hung with snow.

Clouds of Pink
Pamela Love

Clouds of white are often seen,
and so are those of gray.
But clouds of pink will only come
on special springtime days.

Blossoms on a cherry tree
float before our eyes,
letting us reach out and touch
a part of Easter's sky.

And when at last their time is done,
they do not disappear;
our memories hold those petals pink
till once more Easter's near.

Photograph © Hang Dinh/Shutterstock

Rebirth

Kathryn Slasor

The snowflakes melt upon the grass;
a breeze, the tulips now embrace.
Unwilling, winter closed the door,
and spring rushed in to take its place.

The jonquil lifts its golden head;
the lily glistens, pure and white.
Earth's creatures wake from idle sleep
to thus behold the wondrous sight.

The dawn streams forth from eastern sky;
the leaves unfurl with life anew.

God's presence now is manifest
within each drop of sparkling dew.

The cross upon the hill is bare;
the yawning grave, of victory cries.
A love, unmeasured yet by man,
ordained the Son of God to rise.

New life, new hope, new Easter dawn—
rebirth of nature and of man.
He lives and reigns forevermore,
fulfilling God's eternal plan.

Easter

Ruth H. Underhill

Easter . . . the time of joy and rebirth.
You can see it everywhere—
in the crimson tulips swaying,
in the lily pure and fair.

Easter . . . the time of refreshment.
You can sense it in the air—
the fragrance of the daffodil
unfolded with tender, special care.

Easter . . . the time of awakening.
Before your wondering eyes,
yesterday 'twas gray and drear,
but today, a colorful surprise!

Easter . . . the time of renewing—
when the feeling of love abides,
the song of a bird speaks cheerfulness
and friendships securely are tied.

SPRING DANCE *by Diane Phalen. Image © Diane Phalen.*

An April Rain
Ralph Waldo Emerson

April, cold with dropping rain,
willows and lilacs brings again,
the whistle of returning birds,
and the trumpet-lowing of the herds.
The scarlet maple-keys betray
what potent blood hath modest May,
what fiery force the earth renews,
the wealth of forms, the flush of hues;
what joy in rosy waves outpoured
flows from the heart of love, the Lord.

Easter Colors
Reginald Holmes

The earth is bright at Easter
and lovely to behold.
The dawn is pink and orchid;
the sunset, red and gold.
Tulips are dressed in crimson
to match the robin's breast;
blue crocus petals rival
the distant mountain crest.
On hills the green is blending
with valleys down below,
as flocks of sheep are grazing,
their coats as white as snow.
And brightly in the distance,
the golden sunlight shines
on silvery lakes and rivers
that nestle in the pines.
Then after springtime showers
have fallen from on high,
God adds the final touch—
a rainbow in the sky.

New Life at Eastertime

Diane Dean White

Years ago at a car show, surrounded by all kinds of booths offering an array of items for sale, my eyes fell upon a variety of unique birdhouses. They were made out of a fine polished wood with a license plate that fit over the top as a roof. I sought out one with a license plate from my home state and the year of my high school graduation. We hung the birdhouse outside our front door so visitors would notice it. At first, the birds just flew by it. It was just a decorative birdhouse, I reasoned.

A few weeks before Easter, though, I heard some chirping outside. A bird, possibly a finch, was flying around the birdhouse. I listened as she sang and fluttered. It seemed as though the sunshine was, that very moment, bringing the spring flowers and sounds of the new season.

A few days later, I heard another sound—little peeps and the sounds of baby birds! I was amazed to think this decorative birdhouse was actually being used to raise a little winged family. Soon, I knew, the mother bird would push them out to learn to fly and be on their own.

With the sounds of spring in the air and this precious guest and her babies outside our window, I thought about another mother. As a young woman, Mary was told she would give birth to the King of kings. She was obedient to God, and Christ was born. When Jesus was a young man, Mary had to allow Him room to grow and go out on His own. One day, thinking Him lost in a crowd, she found Him in the temple. When she questioned what He had been doing, He told her He was doing His Father's business. Although He was quite young, she had to let Him go.

His thirty-three years of life on earth were consumed with teaching, preaching, and performing miracles. On a dark Friday, the Babe born to Mary gave the world His greatest gift. He was taken to a wooden cross, where He was nailed and tortured, spit upon, and left to die. Yet He spoke these words: "Father, forgive them; for they know not what they do."

Friday was a dark day, a day of weeping for Christ's followers. But on Sunday morning, the sun shone and the tomb was open and He was alive. Later, Christ ascended into heaven, and many who doubted came to believe.

Just like the mother bird has to allow her babies to go on their own, Mary had to allow Jesus to do what God had ordained, letting Him go. And though her pain at His death on the cross must have been great, God's plan was grander than she could ever have fathomed. Through Him we can begin again and learn to fly. On Easter Sunday, we celebrate His Resurrection and the new life we are offered through Him.

Family Recipes

Daffodil Cake

1 cup plus 2 tablespoons cake flour, divided
1½ cups granulated sugar, divided
1⅓ cups egg whites (whites of about 8 eggs)
1¼ teaspoons cream of tartar
¼ teaspoon salt
½ teaspoon vanilla extract
½ teaspoon almond extract
4 well-beaten egg yolks
1 teaspoon lemon extract
Lemon Icing (recipe follows)

Preheat oven to 325°F. In a medium bowl, sift 1 cup flour and ½ cup sugar; set aside. In a large bowl, beat egg whites until frothy. Add cream of tartar and salt; beat until stiff but still glossy. Fold in remaining 1 cup sugar a little at a time. Fold in vanilla and almond extracts. Gradually sift flour-sugar mixture over top of batter. Fold in gently; divide batter in half. In a small bowl, blend egg yolks, 2 tablespoons cake flour, and lemon extract; fold into half of cake batter. Alternately layer the two batters in an ungreased 10-inch tube pan. Bake until top springs back when lightly touched and toothpick inserted into center comes out clean, 55 minutes to 1 hour. Invert pan on wire rack; cool at least 1 hour. Unmold cake; pour icing over top and drizzle down the side. Sift 2 tablespoons confectioners' sugar over top of cake. Makes 12 to 16 servings.

Lemon Icing

1 pound plus 2 tablespoons confectioners' sugar, divided
¼ cup milk
¼ cup lemon juice
yellow food coloring

In a small bowl, sift 1 pound confectioners' sugar. Gradually stir in milk and lemon juice to a smooth consistency, thin enough to drizzle down sides of cake. Tint icing pale yellow by adding several drops of food coloring.

Sunday Baked Ham

½ fully cooked bone-in ham
    (about 5 pounds)
1 8-ounce can jellied cranberry sauce
¼ cup brown sugar

2 tablespoons frozen orange juice
    concentrate
1 tablespoon vinegar
⅛ teaspoon ground cloves
    whole cloves

Preheat oven to 325°F. Place ham on a rack in a roasting pan. Trim excess fat or tough rind from top of ham with a sharp knife, leaving ¼-inch layer of fat. Score fat in a diamond pattern. Bake uncovered 30 minutes. During last 10 minutes, in a small saucepan, combine cranberry sauce, brown sugar, orange juice concentrate, vinegar, and ground cloves. Bring to a boil; reduce heat. Simmer 2 minutes, stirring constantly. Remove ham from oven. Insert whole cloves where points in scoring meet. Brush glaze on ham; return to oven. Bake 1 hour, brushing with glaze every 15 minutes. Let rest 10 minutes before slicing. Makes 6 servings.

Broccoli-Rice Casserole

1 10-ounce package frozen,
    chopped broccoli
1 8-ounce package Velveeta, cubed
½ cup chopped celery
¼ cup chopped onion

2 tablespoons butter
1 10.5-ounce can condensed cream of
    mushroom soup
½ cup milk
2½ cups cooked rice

Preheat oven to 350°F. Cook broccoli according to package directions; drain well. Add cheese cubes; stir and set aside. In a medium skillet, sauté celery and onion in butter until tender but not brown. In a large bowl, combine cream of mushroom soup and milk; mix well. Stir in rice, broccoli-cheese mixture, and vegetables. Spoon mixture into a 2-quart casserole dish. Bake 40 to 45 minutes or until thoroughly heated. Makes 6 to 8 servings.

The Day of Easter
Ray I. Hoppman

Something more vibrant in church bells that ring,
something more joyous in hymns that we sing,
something more fervent in prayers that we raise,
something so different from average days.
Sunshine or rainfall, the day is aglow,
something to strengthen our faith here below,
something that's special in sermons we hear,
bringing a message of comfort and cheer.
Something so peaceful and something so calm—
the Sunday that follows the Day of the Palm,
greater in beauty than the tree and the bloom;
the Savior has risen and conquered the tomb.
Something transforming this weary old sod,
somehow a clearer awareness of God,
something more binding to family and friends—
that glorious something the Easter Day sends.

Easter in Our Town
Earle J. Grant

Easter in our town
is a beautiful time
with snowy lilies,
church bells' chime.
Easter in our town
means egg-hunt thrills,
downy bunnies, new clothes,
dogwoods frosting hills.

Easter in our town
means greening swards
and counters featuring
lovely greeting cards
that proclaim once more
the blessed old story
that the tomb is empty—
Christ reigns in glory!

Easter Ritual
Berniece Ayers Hall

Six cups line the tabletop—
six magic-colored pools.
Six pure-white eggs sit in a row,
along with printed rules.

Each egg, in turn, dipped in the cup
becomes a lovely hue—
amethyst or emerald
or gold or red or blue.

Lift gently, hands—each rainbow tint
an Easter message tells,
and precious is the ritual
of Easter egg pastels!

A Basketful of Eggs
Eileen Spinelli

We dyed our eggs green and blue,
sunny yellow, purple too.
And then we brought them one by one
to neighbors. It was so much fun
to see the sparkle in their eyes
because of such a small surprise.

We learned that day, in early spring,
that kindness is a simple thing—
that smiles and eggs can
make hearts sing.

Photograph © grintan/Shutterstock

Hopping Down the Bunny Trail

Lynne Cobb

One warm spring afternoon, when I was a little girl, my first-grade class returned from our afternoon recess. It was the day before Easter break, so visions of Easter dinner, wearing our new Easter clothes, eating jellybeans, and riding our bikes filled our minds.

While we had been outside, a visitor had stopped in our classroom! As we filed back in for the last hour of the day, a hush came over us. Little baskets stuffed with Easter grass and jellybeans were on each desk, along with bunny-shaped cookies and a glass of punch. Even more exciting were the little rabbit footprints that encircled our desks. The Easter Bunny had quietly sneaked into the school.

Every Easter, I remember that magical day. As a mother, I had often thought how much fun it would be to recreate something similar for my children. But the evening before Easter was usually filled with assembling and hiding their baskets, making sure their clothing was ready for church in the morning, and making something special for breakfast. A partially chewed carrot representing the bunny's visit was the extent of our creative efforts.

One year, however, I decided to make a set of rabbit pawprints by the kitchen table where our children left a carrot out for the Easter Bunny.

I wondered what was used for the pawprints in my classroom. Grabbing a bag of flour from the pantry, I thought, "This will work!" Dumping some flour in a bowl, I got on all fours and started making pawprints on the rug.

I stood back to observe my handiwork, satisfied. I brushed off my hands, emptied the leftover flour into the trash, and washed the bowl.

When I turned from the sink, I was stunned. The prints had vanished! It was then I noticed our beagle licking his chops.

Back to the pantry I went, digging for something I knew the dog wouldn't eat. "What else is white and powdery?" I yawned. It was nearly midnight.

"Baking soda! That will work! I know the dog won't eat that, and it will freshen the rug too," I mused, grabbing the box.

I got back to work. "Two prints done, two to go," I thought, sprinkling the soda into the palm of my hand.

Very sleepy and impatient to be finished, I started to rush. A clump of baking soda was blocking the pour spout. Squishing and mashing the box as quietly as I could, I felt the chunk break off inside the cardboard container. Suddenly a massive amount of baking soda shot out of the box top and all over the two prints.

"Oh no!" I cried, trying to scoop up the enormous mess. It was much too late to run the vacuum cleaner, and I knew that the perfect prints were gone forever. So, not knowing what else to do, I made pawprints—huge pawprints—from the half box of baking soda on the floor. The prints were double the size of my feet, and this time I only made two.

"I will tell the children that the bunny ate his carrots while standing on his back feet," I justified, trying to clean up the rest of the mess. Not only did these pawprints look nothing like the ones I remembered in school, they looked nothing like any animal I had ever seen. I hoped that our children wouldn't visualize a Bigfoot Easter Bunny and be terrified of Easter in future years.

In the morning, we heard the squeals of delight as our children discovered the pawprints, half-eaten carrot, and baskets of goodies.

"Mommy, look! The Easter Bunny was here!" they exclaimed.

"Wow, well, look at that. He sure was here," I agreed.

"We didn't think he was that big, Mommy," they said, trying to picture how big this rabbit must be.

We took several pictures of the pawprints, and I laugh every time I see the photos, even all these years later. Apparently, there was no long-term trauma induced—just good memories of the year the giant Easter Bunny hopped in for a visit.

Photograph © Friedrich Strauss/Gap Photos Ltd.

The Nicest Memory

Patricia Rose Mongeau

I have many happy memories
of days when I was small,
but I think Easter's just about
the nicest of them all.

It always was exciting
on Easter morn to find
eggs and sweets and other treats
the bunny left behind.

I always will remember
the year when I was six,
when there inside my basket
was a little yellow chick!

Though many childhood memories
are pleasant to recall,
I think Easter's just about
the nicest of them all!

Finding Easter Eggs

Frances Bowles

When I was only six, my dear,
and orchards were in bloom,
I used to look for Easter eggs
in every place and room.
When I was only six, my dear,
I searched from east to west
until I found some Easter eggs
hid in a rabbit's nest.
The rabbit was no longer there,
but she had left for me

some bright and shining colored eggs
beneath a snow-white tree.
Now that I am no longer six,
I journey back each spring
to find the rabbit's cozy nest
and hear a robin sing.
And there again I find the eggs
of red and green and blue.
And once again I keep the faith
of Eastertime—don't you?

Discoveries

Dan A. Hoover

Little grandson, not quite two,
Easter morn is here.
You're bundled up to search for eggs,
wearing bunny ears.
Round the red azalea bushes,
glorious with bloom—
springtime's generous beauty,
nature's outdoor room—
I'll watch as you discover "nests,"
squealing with surprise.
What is half so precious as
a baby's laughing eyes?

Baby's First Easter

Garnett Ann Schultz

She'll have the sweetest bonnet
and a dress of softest blue,
a matching ribbon for her hair
and shoes all white and new.
Old Peter Rabbit won't forget
a basket filled with toys
and lots of brightly colored eggs
to bring her Easter joys.

She'll be our brightest Easter flower
to make our day worthwhile.
We're sure she'll have a happy heart,
a precious baby smile.
Her little eyes will light with joy
this lovely springtime morn,
and roses for a little "Miss,"
her bonnet will adorn.

She'll never know the meaning of
the many things we've done—
the basket we tied with a bow,
the extra bits of fun.
She's much too small to understand
why things must be just so,
and why she's all dressed up today,
we're sure she cannot know.

And yet this darling little girl
in Easter bonnet fair
will surely feel the tender love
we've tried to give and share.
So very small and very dear
this first bright Easter Day,
she's Easter happiness complete
in such a precious way.

Christ Is Risen!
Evelyn Weeks Taylor

Easter morning! Easter morning!
Cherub choirs sweetly sing.
Little faces scrubbed and shining,
"Christ is risen!" their voices ring.

Little chapels, widely scattered,
great cathedrals, spries so tall—
yet the echo, "Christ is risen!"
rises skyward from them all.

Easter Joy
Merle Marquis Frank

Let children's happy voices sing
and glad, exultant church bells ring.
Let flowers waft perfume on high
and people's praises rend the sky.
For hope has sprung from empty tomb
which sealed for sin and death their doom;
and man, estranged from God, restored
because He bore our sins, my Lord.
a fruitful life He offered me
when He made death so glorious be.
His love, His work, His power, His way
He gave on Resurrection day.

Photograph © Masterfile

Bits & Pieces

And He departed from our sight that we might return to our heart and there find Him. For He departed, and behold, He is here.
—*St. Augustine*

Oh, Easter anthems gladly sing,
let all the bells from towers ring
and sun dispel with brightening rays
the darkness of the Passion days!
—*Josephine Rice Creelman*

Tomb, thou shalt not hold Him longer;
death is strong, but life is stronger;
stronger than the dark, the light;
stronger than the wrong, the right.
—*Phillips Brooks*

In the bonds of death He lay
Who for our offense was slain;
but the Lord is risen today.
Christ hath brought us life again;
wherefore let us all rejoice,
singing loud, with cheerful voice,
hallelujah!
—Martin Luther

Chime, solemn bells of Easter!
The shadows flee away,
and all the earth is smiling
in the glory of the day.
—Margaret E. Sangster

Praise with hands and voices singing;
praise with verse and chorus ringing.
Christ the Lord is risen today;
He is the Truth, the Life, the Way!
—Carol Penner

For I remember it is Easter morn,
and life and love and peace are
all new-born.
—Alice Freeman Palmer

When the bells ring out at Easter
and the organ starts to play
all those joyful notes of triumph
that belong to Easter Day,
then, with earthly cares receding,
clouds of doubt and fear depart,
rays of hope come shining brightly,
and it's springtime in my heart!
—Cleo King

A Most Unusual Easter Service

Jennie Ivey

For the first time in my life, I wouldn't be in church on Easter Sunday. I'd promised my husband, George, that I would go camping with him and some of our friends that weekend in April to celebrate his birthday. It didn't even cross my mind that it might be Easter.

Only later did I realize my mistake—too late to cancel the trip. "That's all right," I told myself. "You go to church every Sunday. You can take this Sunday off."

But then I kept thinking of what I would be missing: organ music ringing from the rafters, the sweet smell of Easter lilies at the altar, our friends dressed in their spring best, all of us repeating the ancient refrain, "He is risen, risen indeed."

I kept replaying Easter memories: hunting colored eggs in the backyard with my brother as a child, driving five hours home from college to attend church with my parents, posing my children in their new outfits for the annual photo.

Even now, when it was just George and me—empty nesters, sitting shoulder to shoulder in our packed church—Easter was special. I felt guilty about not celebrating.

As soon as we got to Cades Cove Campground in the Great Smoky Mountains National Park, I hurried to the welcome station to ask the ranger if she knew of any groups holding Easter services.

"Not that I've heard," she said.

"What about the churches in Cades Cove?"

The ranger frowned. "If they are, no one's told us," she said, shaking her head as if I'd asked an odd question.

Cades Cove is one of the most popular spots in the park. Every year almost two million visitors travel its eleven-mile loop by car, foot, or bicycle to catch a glimpse of not just the wildlife in the area—the white-tailed deer, coyotes, wild turkey, red foxes, and even the occasional black bear, the symbol of the Great Smoky Mountains—but also its historical roots.

The first settlers came to Cades Cove in the 1820s. They cleared, plowed, and planted the land. They built log cabins and barns and mills that sheltered and sustained them and their descendants for over a hundred years. When the land was purchased to make a national park in the 1930s, these settlers' families moved away. The preserved buildings remain, including Cades Cove's three old churches.

I went back to our campsite. We played Scrabble and had campfire hot dogs for lunch.

"Who's up for a bike ride through Cades Cove?" I asked.

"I'd love to, Jennie."

"Sure."

"Count me in."

We headed off to the village. I pulled over at stop number four on the self-guided tour: the Primitive Baptist church. Maybe someone had posted a notice for a service? Nope. Same with stop number five, the Methodist church. And stop number seven, the Missionary Baptist church.

I'd struck out. There would be no Easter service for me this year.

Sunday morning I awoke at dawn to a heavy fog. George was still asleep, and none of our friends were stirring. I scrawled a note, put it next to the coffeepot, grabbed my bike, and pedaled to Cades Cove.

"Morning," I said to the ranger who was just unlocking the gate. "Happy Easter!"

The new grass in the meadow was fresh with dew. White dogwood blossoms dotted the woods. A doe and her fawn stared at me through the mist.

Three miles in, I came to the charming little Cades Cove Methodist Church. Built in 1902, the white clapboard building had a sheet metal roof and a simple bell tower. It had two doors, one for men and one for women, and both were open.

I slipped inside. Three dozen pews, a massive wooden pulpit, and—in the corner—an ancient piano. "An Easter service should start with a hymn," I thought. "But I'm not much of a pianist, and I only know one hymn by heart."

I sat down and haltingly picked out the notes: "Joyful, joyful, we adore Thee, God of glory, Lord of love . . ." Then I stepped up to the pulpit, where I found a worn leather Bible.

"God bless everyone who opens this book," a note read. I turned the yellowed pages to Luke's Gospel and read the account of the Resurrection—how the women came to the tomb on the third day, shocked to discover it empty.

There, in that empty church, their surprise and bewilderment registered even more with me. I read aloud what the angels said to them: "Why seek ye the living among the dead? He is not here, but is risen . . ."

Cades Cove Methodist Church in Great Smoky Mountains National Park, Tennessee. Photograph © Betty Shelton/Shutterstock

I looked up. A young couple with three small children stood in one of the doorways.

The dad took off his hat. "Excuse me," he said. "We heard the piano. Are you having Easter here today?"

Was I? Easter had come to me all on its own: the blooming dogwoods, the deer, the new grass, the music, the lesson, and, now, others to share it with. Christ had risen and was alive—for the women at the tomb, for me, for us.

"Yes," I said. "Come on in."

I stayed at the pulpit and read the Easter story from Luke out loud; then the daughter suggested her favorite hymn: "Jesus Loves Me." The mom asked if she could lead us in prayer, and we all bowed our heads.

"Thank You, God, for Easter and new friends."

"Amen," we said.

We walked out of the church into the warm spring sun, a day bright with the promise of Easter.

Easter Morn

Louise Lewin Matthews

Easter morn with lilies fair
fills the church with perfumes rare,
as their clouds of incense rise,
sweetest offerings to the skies.
Stately lilies pure and white
flood the darkness with their light.
Bloom and sorrow drift away
on this hallow'd Easter Day
as the lilies, bending low
in the golden afterglow,
bear a message from the sod
to the heavenly towers of God.

Easter Sonnet

J. Harold Gwynne

With flaming sunburst dawns the Easter Day;
the bells ring out, and birds their matins sing
while all the people rise to sing and pray
and greet the sacred festival of spring!
Exultant voices lift in heartfelt praise;
God's servants tell the Resurrection news,
and choral groups their joyous anthems raise.
The radiant Easter lilies row on row
affirm the message of eternal life;
the sanctuary windows softly glow
and speak of heavenly peace beyond the strife.
Above all these—we bless Thee, risen Lord:
Thy glorious name be evermore adored!

The Arrest and Crucifixion
MARK 14:32–46; JOHN 19:16B–18, 29–30

AND THEY CAME TO A PLACE which was named Gethsemane: and he saith to his disciples, Sit ye here, while I shall pray. And he taketh with him Peter and James and John, and began to be sore amazed, and to be very heavy; And saith unto them, My soul is exceeding sorrowful unto death: tarry ye here, and watch. And he went forward a little, and fell on the ground, and prayed that, if it were possible, the hour might pass from him. And he said, Abba, Father, all things are possible unto thee; take away this cup from me: nevertheless not what I will, but what thou wilt.

And he cometh, and findeth them sleeping, and saith unto Peter, Simon, sleepest thou? couldest not thou watch one hour? Watch ye and pray, lest ye enter into temptation. The spirit truly is ready, but the flesh is weak. And again he went away, and prayed, and spake the same words.

And when he returned, he found them asleep again, (for their eyes were heavy,) neither wist they what to answer him. And he cometh the third time, and saith unto them, Sleep on now, and take your rest: it is enough, the hour is come; behold, the Son of man is betrayed into the hands of sinners. Rise up, let us go; lo, he that betrayeth me is at hand.

And immediately, while he yet spake, cometh Judas, one of the twelve, and with him a great multitude with swords and staves, from the chief priests and the scribes and the elders.

And he that betrayed him had given them a token, saying, Whomsoever I shall kiss, that same is he; take him, and lead him away safely. And as soon as he was come, he goeth straightway to him, and saith, Master, master; and kissed him.

And they laid their hands on him, and took him. . . .

AND THEY TOOK JESUS, and led him away. And he bearing his cross went forth into a place called the place of a skull, which is called in the Hebrew Golgotha: Where they crucified him, and two other with him, on either side one, and Jesus in the midst. . . .

Now there was set a vessel full of vinegar: and they filled a spunge with vinegar, and put it upon hyssop, and put it to his mouth.

When Jesus therefore had received the vinegar, he said, It is finished: and he bowed his head, and gave up the ghost.

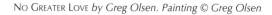

NO GREATER LOVE *by Greg Olsen. Painting © Greg Olsen*

The Resurrection

JOHN 20:1–18

THE FIRST DAY OF THE WEEK cometh Mary Magdalene early, when it was yet dark, unto the sepulchre, and seeth the stone taken away from the sepulchre. Then she runneth, and cometh to Simon Peter, and to the other disciple, whom Jesus loved, and saith unto them, They have taken away the LORD out of the sepulchre, and we know not where they have laid him.

Peter therefore went forth, and that other disciple, and came to the sepulchre. So they ran both together: and the other disciple did outrun Peter, and came first to the sepulchre. And he stooping down, and looking in, saw the linen clothes lying; yet went he not in. Then cometh Simon Peter following him, and went into the sepulchre, and seeth the linen clothes lie, And the napkin, that was about his head, not lying with the linen clothes, but wrapped together in a place by itself. Then went in also that other disciple, which came first to the sepulchre, and he saw, and believed. For as yet they knew not the scripture, that he must rise again from the dead. Then the disciples went away again unto their own home.

But Mary stood without at the sepulchre weeping: and as she wept, she stooped down, and looked into the sepulchre, And seeth two angels in white sitting, the one at the head, and the other at the feet, where the body of Jesus had lain.

And they say unto her, Woman, why weepest thou?

She saith unto them, Because they have taken away my LORD, and I know not where they have laid him. And when she had thus said, she turned herself back, and saw Jesus standing, and knew not that it was Jesus.

Jesus saith unto her, Woman, why weepest thou? whom seekest thou?

She, supposing him to be the gardener, saith unto him, Sir, if thou have borne him hence, tell me where thou hast laid him, and I will take him away.

Jesus saith unto her, Mary.

She turned herself, and saith unto him, Rabboni; which is to say, Master.

Jesus saith unto her, Touch me not; for I am not yet ascended to my Father: but go to my brethren, and say unto them, I ascend unto my Father, and your Father; and to my God, and your God.

Mary Magdalene came and told the disciples that she had seen the LORD, and that he had spoken these things unto her.

Jesus Appears to the Disciples

JOHN 20:19–31

THEN THE SAME DAY AT EVENING, being the first day of the week, when the doors were shut where the disciples were assembled for fear of the Jews, came Jesus and stood in the midst, and saith unto them, Peace be unto you. And when he had so said, he shewed unto them his hands and his side. Then were the disciples glad, when they saw the LORD.

Then said Jesus to them again, Peace be unto you: as my Father hath sent me, even so send I you. And when he had said this, he breathed on them, and saith unto them, Receive ye the Holy Ghost: Whose soever sins ye remit, they are remitted unto them; and whose soever sins ye retain, they are retained.

But Thomas, one of the twelve, called Didymus, was not with them when Jesus came.

The other disciples therefore said unto him, We have seen the LORD. But he said unto them, Except I shall see in his hands the print of the nails, and put my finger into the print of the nails, and thrust my hand into his side, I will not believe.

And after eight days again his disciples were within, and Thomas with them: then came Jesus, the doors being shut, and stood in the midst, and said, Peace be unto you. Then saith he to Thomas, Reach hither thy finger, and behold my hands; and reach hither thy hand, and thrust it into my side: and be not faithless, but believing.

And Thomas answered and said unto him, My LORD and my God.

Jesus saith unto him, Thomas, because thou hast seen me, thou hast believed: blessed are they that have not seen, and yet have believed.

And many other signs truly did Jesus in the presence of his disciples, which are not written in this book: But these are written, that ye might believe that Jesus is the Christ, the Son of God; and that believing ye might have life through his name.

O JERUSALEM *by Greg Olsen. Painting © Greg Olsen*

The Angel on the Stone

J. Harold Gwynne

At break of dawn on Easter Day,
the angel rolled the stone away.
This angel sat upon the stone
with mock derision in his tone.
"He is not here," the angel said.
"The Lord has risen from the dead.
He goes before to Galilee;
there you the risen Christ shall see."
The women's hearts were strangely stirred
to hear the angel's prescient word.

Because He conquered death and grave
and gave Himself, our souls to save,
with faith we sing with latest breath
that life is victor over death.

The Living Lord

Marcia K. Leaser

"Come, see, the tomb is empty—
the stone is rolled away,"
the angel declared loudly
as they came to see that day.

Standing at the entrance, they could
scarce believe their eyes.
It was just as He had told them,
just as had been prophesied.

It had to be that way, you know.
There could be no other plan.
He could not stay within the grave
and be the Rescuer of man.

The First Easter Morning

Henrietta E. Page

In Joseph's rock-hewn sepulcher,
the Crucified One slept,
while out amid the starshine
the mourning Marys wept.
So cold and dark, that sepulcher;
so sad and so sore-hearted,
they, spent with tears and watchful love,
then sorrowing, departed.

At the tomb in which no man had laid,
no ray of light crept through
where lay the "Man of Sorrows,"
the tender heart and true.
When—behold!—the portals opened,
and a great unearthly light
streamed through the rock-bound chamber,
dispersing clouds and night.

And the voice of an archangel
pealed through the silent room—
"Arise, Thy Father calls Thee;
arise from out the tomb."
Jesus awoke, unclosed His eyes
and, rising, loosed the bands
of linen fine, with spices dressed,
from off His face and hands.

His head He bowed in silent prayer,
then raised His eyes above—
"Father I come, if 'tis Thy will;
oh, keep Thou those I love."
Ah, glorious Easter Morning
that saw our Savior rise
with print of spear and wounded hands—
a loving sacrifice!

An Invitation

Joyce Hollyday

*I*n the half-light of dawn, in a graveyard, it might have been tempting to believe that their eyes were playing tricks. But the body the women had come to anoint was indeed gone, and the proclamation rang out through the eeriness and emptiness of the place: "He has risen!"

Mary Magdalene and the other Mary fled from the tomb "with fear and great joy," according to Matthew's account. It was a case of mixed emotions entirely appropriate to the occasion. The women were bursting to tell the news, yet they were afraid of what had been revealed first to them.

Before they ever reached the others, they encountered their risen Lord. He greeted them and then offered them the words of reassurance they most needed to hear: "Do not be afraid."

The words are common in the biblical narrative. At the time of Jesus' birth, another time of uncommon joy and fear, Mary, Joseph, Zacharias, and the shepherds in the fields all received the words as reassurance. "Do not be afraid" was part of Jesus' invitation to Peter to be a follower, and the same words rang out over a storm when the disciples became fearful and an overly brave Peter stepped out to walk on water.

Jesus regularly reminded His followers not to fear their enemies or the uncertainties that lay ahead. He invited three trembling disciples at His Transfiguration to discard their fear, and said to the ruler Jairus at his daughter's healing, "Do not fear, only believe."

After Jesus' crucifixion, fear ran rampant among His followers. Joseph of Arimathea, owner of the tomb, asked Pilate for Jesus' body "secretly for fear of the Jews." Nicodemus came with spices to help prepare the body for burial, but only under the safe cover of night. And the inner circle of Jesus' disciples—who had abandoned and, in Peter's case, even denied their Lord—remained hidden behind closed doors.

Even the authorities who had put Him to death were fearful. Great care was taken to securely seal the tomb. And when the news reached the chief priests that Jesus had risen, they devised a cover-up, offering money to the tomb guards to spread the story Jesus' disciples had come and stolen the body.

Against this fear and fraud was the simple faithfulness of the women who had stood at the cross, watched as the stone was rolled over the tomb, and come at dawn to anoint the body. Their reward was the gift of being witnesses to the Resurrection.

"Do not be afraid" were Jesus' first words to them. The message attended His birth, His ministry, His death, and His Resurrection. And it comes to us today with the same gentle and compelling clarity with which it was offered on that first Easter morning.

There is much around us that is awesome and awful. We know too well the divisions and suffering that plague our world. We have seen that the

authorities in modern times use tactics similar to those employed 2,000 years ago, and many people scheme to play to our fear, destroy our hope, and seal off our joy.

But we have the confidence of our faith. We have seen the risen Lord!

Mary and Mary Magdalene loved with such a perfect love that they shed their fear. Empowered by their faith and their encounter with the risen Christ, they ran on to proclaim what they had seen and what they knew to be true. As Jesus had reminded Jairus, they knew they could not both believe and fear. They were among the first to know the truth that John later put into words: "There is no fear in love; but perfect love casteth out fear" (1 John 4:18).

They challenge us to love and believe—to love Jesus with a perfect love and to believe in the power of His Resurrection. Certainly they grieved and experienced their hope flagging during the dark moments surrounding Jesus' death. But they never lost their faith. It remained a small, steady flame that was fanned to brilliant, bold new life in the light of that Easter dawn.

The women invite you and me to such faith. Their testimony stands through the ages. It is a reminder to "fan into flame the gift of God . . . for

the Spirit God gave us does not make us timid, but gives us power, love and self-discipline" (2 Timothy 1:6–7, NIV). With courage and joy, let us claim that same spirit that dwelt within our sisters, the first witnesses of the Resurrection.

First Appearance

Sara Henderson Hay

In all His resurrected grace,
how easily He might have come
and, meeting Pilate face to face,
stricken him dumb.

How well this Jesus might have stood
suddenly in the city square
and watched the stricken multitude
tremble and stare.

With what immensity of right
He could have come again and thrust
the council into outer night,
the law to dust.

How like the gentle Mary's Son
to put aside the whirlwind reaping
and minister to the need of one
who sought Him, weeping.

How blessed beyond the proudest word
was Mary Magdalene, who came
early unto the tomb and heard
Christ speak her name!

Photograph © aGinger/Shutterstock

Matin

Thelma J. Compton

How quiet was my cathedral
on a sun-struck Easter morn
when I slipped into the forest
at the breaking of the dawn.

How still the woodland creatures;
they must have been at prayer!
The rustle of an oak leaf
as it drifted through the air

was, indeed, the only sound
that broke my meditation
while I sat in silent reverence
of the Father of Creation.

I was wafted to the heavens
with an inward thrill of awe,
looked with muted adoration
on the perfection that I saw.

Suddenly the prayers were over.
The hemlock sighed, "Amen,"
and the glory of an anthem
swelled above the cloistered glen.

The birds joined in the chorus,
loud the alleluias rang
as the woodland world rejoiced
and their Maker's praises sang.

Lowly creatures sang the paean
"Christ, the Savior, risen Lord!"
then a lowly, sinful human
echoed humbly with accord.

The Parable of the Butterfly

Dr. Ralph F. Wilson

*A*s a butterfly soared overhead, one caterpillar said to the other, "You'll never get me up in one of those things."

Yet for every caterpillar the time comes when the urge to eat and grow subsides, and he instinctively begins to form a chrysalis around himself. The chrysalis hardens, and you'd think for all the world that the caterpillar is dead.

But one spring morning the life inside the chrysalis begins to writhe, the top cracks open, and a beautifully formed butterfly emerges. For hours it will stand stretching and drying its wings, moving them slowly up and down, up and down. And then, before you know it, the butterfly glides

aloft, effortlessly riding the currents of the air and alighting on flower after gorgeous flower as if to show off its vivid colors to the bright blossoms.

Somehow, the miracle of the butterfly never loses its fascination for us. Perhaps because the butterfly is a living parable of the promise of resurrection.

On Easter morning the disciples saw Jesus' graveclothes lying on the cold slab. Only the corpse was gone, much like an empty chrysalis deserted by a butterfly. "He is risen as He said," an angel told the incredulous disciples. Later that day He appeared to the disciples and then, over the course of the next few weeks, to as many as

five hundred people at one time. Even "Doubting Thomas" didn't doubt for long that Jesus was really risen from the dead.

A few weeks ago I lost a friend who had become dear to me. Where she had been so full of life, now her body lay still, composed ever-so-carefully by the morticians. I looked at her and thought about my own mortality. One day I too, like her, may fight a losing battle with pain and die.

What do we Christians say in the face of death? There are many mysteries. But two things we know for sure. First, death is an enemy. Away with the sentimentality that vainly seeks to disguise death's insult! But second, and more important, Jesus' Resurrection from the grave is God's proof to us that death is not the end. The empty tomb and Jesus' Spirit within us testify that Easter morning is God's triumph over death. And ultimately, Jesus promised God will raise from the dead those who believe in His Son.

Why do Christians gather on Easter morning? To show off their fine clothes or give a ritual tip of the hat to religion? God forbid! Rather, we gather to celebrate Jesus' victory over death itself. For since He is our Lord and our Savior, His victory is our victory. In celebrating His Resurrection, we celebrate our own assurance of ultimate triumph over death.

Join us this Easter as we celebrate life! And if you look closely Easter morning, you might even see a butterfly alight on the lilies.

The Church Bells Ring on Easter

Fred Toothaker

When the church bells ring on Easter,
there is grandeur in the sound
as they peal out in their clearness
for the many worship-bound.
There's a melody that's haunting me
on this, the Sabbath day,
as I'm beckoned to the temple
where all can meet and pray.
When the church bells toll on Easter,
it's the Lord inviting you
to assemble with your neighbors
and your faith and trust renew.
Tolling bells expressing glory
in the steeples where they ring
are the music from the heaven
where it is that angels sing.
When the church bells ring on Easter,
there is everlasting love
in the message they are bringing
from the Master up above.

Message of the Bells

Dorothy L. Elam

Wake the dawn, bells of Easter,
while the dew is on the flower.
Resurrect for us the story
of that dark and dismal hour.

Softly toll as we remember
how that life with promise filled
began as a weary world rejoiced,
yet ended on Golgotha's hill.

Softly toll throughout the dawn
lest we forget—lest we forget!—
the agony and pain He bore,
the death He met, the crown He wore.

Then sound with joy, O bells of Easter!
Peal in tones both loud and clear!
Tell again of how He rose;
tell the tale so sweet and dear.

Tell how He loosed the chains of death
with power triumphant as ne'er before;
tell the world throughout the years
that Jesus lives forevermore!

Yes! Ring out, O bells of Easter;
tell redemption's story—
ever old, yet ever new.
Tell of Jesus' glory!

Photograph © Dervin Witmer/
Shutterstock

Surveying the Cross

Pamela Kennedy

Easter music usually brings to mind glorious cantatas, richly chorded anthems, and choruses filled with melodic and interwoven "hallelujahs." But this favorite hymn is unique in that it only comprises five notes: A, B, E, F, and G. Simple, yet bold, it is one of the most enduring anthems of the Christian church.

Both the author and composer of this hymn were gifted musically, but they never met, hailing from different countries and generations. Born in Southampton, England, in 1674, Isaac Watts was the eldest of nine children and a prodigy. By the age of thirteen, he had mastered Latin, Greek, French, and Hebrew and had the unusual and, to his father, irritating habit of conversing in rhymes. When the elder Watts threatened to spank his son if he persisted, young Isaac responded, "Oh, Father, do some pity take, and I will no more verses make!"

Fortunately, for all who enjoy beautiful hymns, Isaac broke his promise. As a teenager, he accepted the challenge of composing a new hymn each week for the congregation of his father's church, and even the Reverend Watts was forced to admit that his son had a gift for translating the words of Scripture into song. At first, Isaac only used the words of the Psalms, but as he gained experience, the young composer wrote hymns that translated the experiences and emotions of faith into verses to be sung in church. It was from this perspective that the words of "When I Survey the Wondrous Cross" evolved.

Picturing himself at the foot of the cross, and perhaps imagining the perspective of Mary and John from the Gospels, Isaac described the wonder inspired by the sacrificial love of Jesus. At the time of its writing, this type of hymn was considered radical. Departing from the earliest traditions of church music, critics branded it too emotional and personal. Yet it is those very qualities that have been appreciated by later generations.

When the American composer Lowell Mason discovered Isaac Watts' verses in the mid-nineteenth century, he chose an ancient Gregorian chant as the basis for his hymn tune. Using only five different notes, he created a hauntingly beautiful melody for the words written by the British poet.

In all, Watts wrote over 600 hymns, and Mason composed 1,600 hymn tunes. But "When I Survey the Wondrous Cross" remains one of their few collaborations. It stands as an enduring testimony to the talent and faith of these two men, who, although separated by time and nationality, combined their gifts to give their faith a voice.

When I Survey the Wondrous Cross

Words: Isaac Watts (1674–1748) Music: Lowell Mason (1792–1872)

1. When I sur - vey the won - drous cross
2. For - bid it, Lord, that I should boast,
3. See, from His head, His hands, His feet,
4. Were the whole realm of na - ture mine,

on which the Prince of Glo - ry died;
save in the death of Christ, my God;
sor - row and love flow min - gled down.
that were an of - f'ring far too small;

My rich - est gain I count but loss,
All the vain things that charm me most,
Did e'er such love and sor - row meet,
Love so a - maz - ing, so di - vine,

and pour con - tempt on all my pride.
I sac - ri - fice them all to His blood.
or thorns com - pose so rich a crown?
de - mands my soul, my life, my all.

Ye Heav'ns, Uplift Your Voice
Fifteenth Century Carol

Ye heav'ns, uplift your voice;
sun, moon, and stars, rejoice;
and thou, too, nether earth,
join in the common mirth,
for winter storm, at last,
and rain are over-past;
instead whereof the green
and fruitful palm are seen.
Ye flow'rs of spring, appear;
your gentle heads uprear,
and let the growing seed
enamel lawn and mead.

Ye roses, inter-set
with clumps of violet;
ye lilies white, unfold
in beds of marigold.
Ye birds with open throat,
prolong your sweetest note;
awake, ye blissful quires,
and strike your merry lyres.
For why? Unhurt by death,
the Lord of life and breath,
Jesus, as He foresaid,
is risen from the dead.

The Music of Spring
Kay Hoffman

The winter days are over now;
spring music fills the air.
Robins sing their cheery tunes
from treetops everywhere.
The brooklet's happy chatter's
like small children at their play.
Bullfrog, not to be outdone,
plays bass violin today.
Seeds are stirring 'neath the sod;
buds, bursting in the air.
Ah, yes, discerning ears can hear
spring music everywhere.
From woodland near comes
    rustling sounds
of frisky squirrels at play;

the bunny's hopping on the lawn
in his delightful way.
The honk of wild geese flying north
'neath skies of wind-swept blue,
a laughing lad with kite in hand
tell us that winter's through.
My lagging feet now want to dance,
my heart can't help but sing,
when Maestro Mother Nature plays
her composition "Spring."

Easter's Paradise

Inez Franck

Walking through the flowered cherries,
wonder-topped in pink and white,
looking at the blue-eyed meadows,
feeling dawn's extreme delight—
suddenly my heart is singing
in Easter's paradise.

Picking violets in the woodlands,
listening to the mockingbird,
smelling lanes of apple petals,
knowing miracles occurred—
suddenly my joy is ringing
with Easter bells of love.

ISBN-13: 978-0-8249-1347-2

Published by Ideals Publications
A division of Worthy Media, Inc.
Nashville, Tennessee
www.idealsbooks.com

Printed and bound in the U.S.A.
Printed on Weyerhaeser Lynx. The paper used in this publication meets the minimum requirements of American National Standard for Information Sciences—Permanence of Paper for Printed Materials, ANSI Z39.48-1984.

Publisher, Peggy Schaefer
Editor, Melinda L. R. Rumbaugh
Copy Editors, Rachel Pate and Debra Wright
Designer, Marisa Jackson
Permissions Editor, Kristi West

Cover: Photograph © Artens/Shutterstock
Inside front cover: *Horned Lark & Daffodils* by Susan Bourdet. Artwork courtesy of the artist and Wild Wings (800-445-4833; www.wildwings.com).
Inside back cover: *Ruby's Garden Hummingbird* by Susan Bourdet. Artwork courtesy of the artist and Wild Wings (800-445-4833; www.wildwings.com).

Sheet Music for "When I Survey the Wondrous Cross" by Dick Torrans, Melode, Inc. Additional art credits: Pages 1, 22, 36, 60, and back cover art by Kathy Rusynyk. The following pages contain art © [the artist]/Shutterstock.com: 5, Padmayogini, Magnia; 6, Victoria Sergeeva; 14, lozas; 16, Zhanna Smolyar; 20, Angie Makes, Mike Demidov; 24–25, egluteskarota; 26, Mariika; 28, Oksana Alekseeva, Curly Pat; 31, Dzujen; 38–39, Suchkova Anna; 40, Angie Makes; 42–47, Oaurea, Megin; 50, Iliveinoctober; 56–57, Liliya Shlapak; 59, Le Panda; 63, Regina Jershova; 64, anemad.

Join the community of *Ideals* readers on Facebook at: www.facebook.com/IdealsMagazine
Readers are invited to submit original poetry and prose for possible use in future publications. Please send no more than four typed submissions to: Magazine Submissions, Ideals Publications, 2630 Elm Hill Pike, Suite 100, Nashville, Tennessee 37214. Manuscripts will be returned if a self-addressed stamped envelope is included.

ACKNOWLEDGMENTS:

BORLAND, HAL. "The Root of the Matter" from Borland Country by Hal Borland Copyright © 1947, 1948, 1949, 1950, 1951, 1952, 1953, 1956, 1971 by Hal Borland. Reprinted by permission of Frances Collin. HOLLYDAY, JOYCE. "An Invitation" reprinted with permission from Sojourners, Copyright © April 1987, (800) 714-7474, www.sojo.net. IVEY, JENNY. "A Most Unusual Easter Service" from *Guideposts Magazine*, Copyright © March 2013 by Guideposts. All rights reserved. Used by permission. PENNER, CAROL. "Praise with hands and voices singing . . ." excerpted from a poem titled "Joyful Easter Call to Worship," Copyright © Carol Penner at www.carolpenner.typepad.com. All rights reserved. Used by permission. WILSON, RALPH F. "The Parable of the Butterfly" Copyright © Ralph F. Wilson, www.joyfulheart.com. All rights reserved. Used by permission. OUR THANKS to the following authors or their heirs: Faye Adams, Frances Bowles, Lynne Cobb, Thelma J. Compton, Dorothy L. Elam, Merle Marquis Fran, Inez Franck, Earl J. Grant, Virginia Borman Grimmer,

J. Harold Gwynne, Berniece Ayers Hall, Sara Henderson Hay, Kay Hoffman, Reginald Holmes, Dan A. Hoover, Ray I. Hoppman, Pamela Kennedy, Marcia K. Leaser, Norma West Linder, Pamela Love, Louise Lewin Matthews, Patricia Rose Mongeau, Garnett Ann Schultz, Kathryn Slasor, Vera Keevers Smith, Eileen Spinelli, Evelyn Weeks Taylor, Fred Toothaker, Ruth H. Underhill, Lorna Volk, Mary Weeks, Diane Dean White. Scripture quotations, unless otherwise indicated, are taken from King James Version (KJV). Scripture quotations marked NIV are taken from the HOLY BIBLE, NEW INTERNATIONAL VERSION®. Copyright © 1973, 1978, 1984 Biblica. Used by permission of Zondervan. All rights reserved.

Every effort has been made to establish ownership and use of each selection in this book. If contacted, the publisher will be pleased to rectify any inadvertent errors or omissions in subsequent editions.